I0756253

FINISHING LINE PRESS
www.finishinglinepress.com

SHOULD HAVE KNOWN

poems by

Linda Arntzenius

Finishing Line Press
Georgetown, Kentucky

SHOULD HAVE KNOWN

In memory of my adored sister Frances Sleith (1944-2008)
and all the other old souls in my life

ISBN 979-8-89990-477-6 First Edition

ACKNOWLEDGMENTS

Versions of several poems in this collection have been published in the following journals:

Paterson Literary Review: Peace Offering
Potpourri: Self Portrait
Slant: Give and Take
TCNJ Writers Conference Chronicle: Pygmalion and Galatea, Choosing Artwork for a Friend
Up & Under: Remembering Sally Topps
U.S.1 Weekly Summer Fiction Issue: Quaker Road
US1 Worksheets: Invitation, Narcissus, No One out Today, Stilled Life, Return, Storm Over the Black Isle
Non-Binary Review: I Watch My Father Shaving

Publisher: Leah Huete de Maines
Editor: Christen Kincaid
Cover Art: Shutterstock: Eugene_Photo
Author Photo: Michelle Gantner
Cover Design: Elizabeth Maines McCleavy

Order online: www.finishinglinepress.com
also available on amazon.com

Author inquiries and mail orders:
Finishing Line Press
PO Box 1626
Georgetown, Kentucky 40324
USA

Contents

Narcissus

Honeymoon, Glen Shiel, Scotland

I should have known
when my love could not resist
the stream that skeltered
off the mountain
rounded rocks and crevices
until broken by a hollow
forced to pause
where beaded bubbles rose
through aquamarine—
as he flung off his clothes and plunged into the froth,
wondering how I could resist.

Then, when he was done
and gripping me, naked and shivering,
I fully clothed—
a contrast so thrilling
we rode the mountain long
as sheep looked chastely on.

I should have known then,
when he told me: *good as it was*
it didn't compare to his icy dip.

He spoke his truth
while I, schooled in metaphor,
deciphered the calligraphy of water beads
patterning his thighs
and even now hear the rush
of mountain water
in my ears.

Pygmalion and Galatea

He:
Each day he worked
boldly at first, chipping, hammering
seeking the imagined form
the long white shapely arm
the perfect breast

—how he would teach
the heart to love
the limbs to caress
what sweet sounds would emanate from this throat
these lips—

softly smoothing
until at last
his Galatea stepped down
blinked at the untidy atelier
as if surprised by marble-grit and dust
she seemed to say: *what were you thinking?*
with no more than a glance
as she fled…

She:
. . . not to know where your body
ends and the rock begins . . .

the sheer oppress of white oblivion
and yet there's safety here
and solitude
                    a quiet peace
until his chipping purpose
the hammering intent
of hope and promise

—expectation
weightier than alabaster

—heaviest of all
his cow-eyed adoration.

Self Portrait

I am clutter, cluttering his streamlined life
with children, furniture, dinner parties, bric-a-brac.

Second-hand store rescues, auction finds
bind his legs with tapestries and ribbons,
stuff his mouth with decades of dust.

He wades among my leather-bound volumes,
stumbles over whatnots and Windsor chairs,
baroque barricades between us—

the quilter and the logical positivist,
male and female, dextra and sinistra,
straight and infuriatingly curvy
in an endless Pythagorean dance of opposites.

I synthesize. He analyzes and dissects
—splitting hairs that I would twist into yarn.

Give and Take

En amour, il y en a toujours un qui souffre et l'autre qui s'ennuie.
—Balzac

One more cup of tea and then I'm off.
—This from the woman who
before they were married
drank no tea at all, had no use
for a nightcap of MacCallan,
could not sleep without Bartok or Hindemith,
hardly slept at all and made a hash
of the bedclothes when she did.

While he delighted in gentler melodies,
bedded down blissfully at nine,
addicted to his nightcap and early morning Lapsang.

Now he is the one who pads through the night
with Mendelssohn, Brahms and Mahler,
while she breathes deep, barely disturbs the covers.

—A puzzling exchange that leaves him
rueful of what he wished to share
        of what he dared to wish.

After His Depression

Life should be easy
and yet . . .
there is grief
for years
lost to grief
empty pages
in the family album
where babies
unconceived
might have been.

In closets
sorrows linger
like the scent
of orange blossom
in a June bouquet
withered now
and stored
with ribbons
in a box.

Epiphany

You're not taking that old thing, he says.
And she sees the rocker with new clarity.
Scars of autumn mold, ravages of insects,
neat little worm-holes—a filigree city
of half tunnels roughening the wood.

Sitting on the back porch, familiar,
she had missed its decline
toward the kind of sorry cast-off
usually found in Salvation Army stores
discarded by dead people's relatives
in a hurry to move on.

They'd bought the rocker together
even before they'd had any kids.
A kind of goofy, old-fashioned thing to do.
And then they grew into it (at least she did).
Nursed her babies, rocked alone while he
worked late, went to conferences, consulted with colleagues.

Now his efforts have paid off.
He is moving on. Moving up.

She turns to where he alone moves unfettered
sorting, discarding, ruthlessly focused.
How grubby it all is, thickened with their life.
The cracked cup where their youngest lost a tooth.
Inherited tapestries, mismatched,
loose threads just begging to be pulled
to unravel and return to friendly chaos.

The kitsch tablecloth, a gift from crazy Lori.
How they'd laughed at its bad taste.
Get rid of it, he'd said.

Compelled to look again at everything,
she moves from packing-case to mirror,
discovers lines and blemishes in her own face.

This stark *gestalt* is a gift there is no undoing.
Just imagine, she tells herself.

Among the bulging packages,
he stands as flat as a paper doll.

It would take no skill, no sleight of hand
to fold the paper arms onto themselves
to concertina the legs up and over the torso
collapse the dainty origami into a neat
little package, postcard size.

All she really needs is one small envelope.
A lick, a short trip to the mailbox
and a sweet plop,
before the slow, delicious
beginning to unpack.

Best Friends Forever

Reality is a cliché from which we escape by metaphor
—Wallace Stevens

Eleven
and galloping limber
down the steep meadow
at the edge of the woods
behind the old slag heap.
Ann and me
our growing pains forgot
every sinew stretched towards a breathless tumble
into the long grass, after our full tilt canter.
Slapping our own backsides
into a *giddy-up*, we inhabit the skins
of the young colts we long to be
neigh our heads off, uninhibitedly,
because we are young,
because we
alone
of all the world,
know it is spring.

Seventeen
and iridescent damselflies
on blood-pulsed gossamer,
our every move an utterance
catch us if you dare.

Twenty-one
glazed-hard as raku-fired clay
clinking from the potter's kiln
—oh the yearnings of summer.

Twenty-two
and parting now with promises to write,
leaving home in brand-new suits
shoes, jobs, luggage,

one-way tickets to London for
bright new lives—twin rose petals
adrift as anchorless boats.

Thirty now
and walking in our own gardens
tending the tomato sets in August
every other plant in seed, taut as parchment
Love-in-a-Mist, cracking pods ready to burst,
to spill upon the whole ripening earth.

Thirty-eight
and heavy again with child
grown kin to all that's meek
having to yield, become pliant
having to wait, become patient,
accepting of all that is to come
the clutching and the letting go.

Through years that pass too swift for counting
we wear each metaphor—of love
and death, betrayal and divorce,
hurt and anger, forgiveness and kindness,
laughter and joy.

Winter finds two rocking crones
with fireside cats and comfort in the thought
my clichéd life is also yours.

Choosing Artwork for a Friend

I'd choose the girl with the punched-tin face,
Medusa dreadlocks in bows, hammered
from an old oil drum in Haiti.

But Ingrid likes pretty with precise
colors that don't bleed,
delicate peaches and sage greens.

Like this genteel patio planter
handprinted with hummingbirds
and honeysuckle.

So, I should ignore the carved-wood fetishes from Mali
and the gaudy block-prints from Rajasthan.

Likewise pass on Oaxacan molas and Romany
cutwork, and steer towards those dainty wall plaques

and dried flower arrangements, complete
with changing slogans for each month of year.

Or must I? Wrap up Miss Medusa please—
that teenage pout, those wayward braids, surely
a parting gift to be remembered by.

Dream House of Desire

I never painted dreams, I painted my own reality.
—Frida Kahlo

Will there be gargoyles and a folly, a ruined tower, a rivulet,
a bridge above a weeded pond with waterlilies blowing?

All these and more, my dear.

Will there be lawns and hedgerows, nesting birds,
terraces with wrought iron gates, stone lions and a fountain?

Let there be unicorns and panthers, monkeys and guavas,
figtrees, pomegranates, parrots and shawls.

Will there be weeping willows, copper beeches, swans on the lake?

There shall be spinning wheels and strawberries, and
views of distant hills.

Doors without locks, windows without shades?

Corridors and casements standing wide.

Fruit trees in an orchard?

Ringed round with thorn and Spanish bayonet.

Only the mirror sees
beyond these silent, unbetraying eyes
the dream house of desire
no man dare enter.

Off the Shelf

They sit like cans of soup upon the shelf.
Unwritten lines await their space upon the page.

Here's one about youth, how it was squandered.
Ruined love, ditto. In back, a rumination on the fetus
hooked like a winkle from its shell.

How about this fine mulligatawny of romance. Too spicy?
The alphabet soup of childhood then.
Orphaned letters going begging.

There's always the parental favorite, corn chowder.
A wee bit knobby and hard to digest, but
like a good Scots Broth, it will improve with keeping.

The sweet and sour of motherhood, perhaps?
An earthy flavor not for every taste.

The *Vichysoisse* of city life—cool and perfectly proportioned.

The iced *gazpacho* of a summer's love affair, ambiguity on the tongue.

Let's start with a clear consommé, the stock and simmer of a life.

I Watch My Father Shaving

My father shaves on Wednesdays the half-shut day.
With meticulous care, he oils the whetstone,
clips the leather strop to the towel-rail,
opens the cut-throat razor, lathers the soap.

After the rush of water comes the scuff
of badger-brush on bristled skin. Then,
the blade I have been warned against.
Tool for suicide, murder, piracy—instrument of intimacy.

But I am young, permitted yet to linger
like a woman outside the Holy of Holies,
unacknowledged as he moves through this spare prelude
toward the crescendo of his good, his going-into-town suit.

I loiter at the doorway until he sees me, sends me off
with three big pennies to squander in Fordyce's sweetshop,
the only shop that doesn't close this afternoon
when the town folds up like my father's razor.

This afternoon, this quiet ritual, is all *his* purpose.
Smooth, he is no longer the crumpled man I clamber on,
fuss with his thinning hair and scratchy mustache,
whose craggy face I paint with Mum's old lipsticks.

Peace Offering

Sometimes, when Dad had been to McClafferty's,
he'd bring home fish suppers as a peace offering.

We prayed our mother would approve.
She could be won over by a special fish from Lenzi's

Gino's own fried haddock in breadcrumbs
instead of the usual batter, already soggy

with vinegar and soaked through
the neat brown paper parcel—

even through several layers of *The Glasgow Herald*
that kept the bundle warm inside Dad's thin overcoat.

From the back bedroom, we'd be roused by the aroma
yet scarcely breathe, lie taut as wire, listening

for signs the gift was to be sanctified
with plates, knives & forks, a pot of tea.

Always touch and go, for if it was payday
and he'd staggered in drunk, Mum could just as easily
toss the bundle out the window, as set the table.

As soon as we heard that magic clink, we'd be up
tiptoeing down the long dark lobby

towards the lighthouse of the kitchen
the savor of salty whiskery kisses,
the steaming optimism of deep-fried fish.

Return

Asleep inside the mountain two decades long,
she awoke, ravenous.

Her jaw was clamped tight.
Her teeth were out of practice,
her stomach hollow, her bowels cavernous.

Taking a long deep breath, she plunged into the stream.

Water refreshed her. She bathed in it
drank deep of it, felt nerves soothe,
cells plump, fibers moisten.

When the blood ran from her eyes.
she stood and began to run.

Perspectives

Prose Poems after Victoria Chang's Obits

1 Time

Sucked into silence in the unmarked moment, the housefly has dropped to the sill. Trapped between pane and screen, the starlit moth has ceased its wingbeat. Skin cells have settled as dust on the sunshade and a curdle of fat has risen to rest at the surface of the milk. As the smoke rises up, as the limb slips down, as the dripping tap deposits its residue, so the yeast devours the last granule of sugar and farts into the sticky dough of our daily bread.

2 Moving on

I took all my quacking ducklings and put them into one of my many baskets. Then I took all my baskets and lined them up in a single row. They made perfect targets for shooting practice. When none but one was left intact, I took all the blasted remnants and placed them into the last basket standing, alongside the ducklings, as it happened. The ducklings were silent now. I took this last of my baskets and set it adrift in the garden pond. For a time, it sailed gaily between the waterweed and the floating lilies. Being tightly packed, it took some time to succumb to the press of water all around. I waited. I watched. Then with a light step and an even lighter heart, I washed my hands of this place.

3 Exploration

There was no denying he was dirty. His long fingernails were caked black. There was no denying she was exquisitely clean, her skin as smooth and clear as a child's. This contrast charged their lovemaking. At least in the beginning. It was only later that she discovered how ill-adept he was at making love, that she had in fact been making love alone, thrilling herself with possibilities created from her own imagination—moved by her own body's youthful athleticism, in sharp relief against his weak limbs and dull sallow skin. She exulted as he responded to her caress. This was new territory. This is what made her dizzy with disgust. If only it could go on forever. If only he hadn't insisted on kissing her.

4 Burnt Toast
This morning, I burnt the last two slices of bread in the toaster. They popped up too soon and so I popped them down again then walked off to read a poem. When I got back smoke was coming out of the toaster. I slathered butter on anyway and smooshed a banana on top. The banana was just about turning black, so it seemed appropriate. The crisp charcoal contrasted wonderfully with the soft overripe fruit. One bite and I was back in our old Glasgow tenement, holding the poker over the kitchen fire, a slice of Mother's Pride stuck on the end of it above the flames. That's how we did it then.

Golden

The golden lion parades the sunlit border.
His golden mane is garlanded with flowers.

His golden majesty surveys the sweet disorder—
goldfinches among sunflower heads
swallowtails flitting from anemone
to zinnia, sneezeweed to yarrow.

Evening primroses prepare to unfold
moonflowers soon will add their glow.

All whisper to the golden lion, all bow their heads.
How grand it must be to be the golden one.

O'Keeffe in New Mexico

When I got to New Mexico it was mine, it was mine as soon as
I saw it.
—Georgia O'Keeffe (1887-1986)

Fill space in a beautiful way, said your teacher.
And so, you started pretty
until New Mexico hit you
with its stark plains like ocean
and you started over with charcoal and black paint.

Because there were no flowers you picked up bones
first a horse's skull, then a cow's
they pleased you—white bones against a hot blue sky—
and you had to have something to take back to Lake George
for those interminable summers on the Stieglitz farm.

If I paint it big the men will have to look at it, you said.
Painters who'd never crossed the Hudson
who'd never seen the West—were made to stare
into the rubbery pubescence of Jack-in-the-Pulpit
—discover among the desert's shifting shapes
and waters roiling the arroyo: The Great American Landscape.

Stilled Life

—from a photograph of Elizabeth's dining room in The Hague

In an alchemy of pure Vermeer, oak transmutes
to ebony with only eggshell glints to confirm
a table laden with dishes for the hubbub of family
who will never disturb this perfect Dutch interior.

Inspect this room. Look for an augur
of what is to come. As if from a photograph
we could read the future as well as the past.
As if, in being still, we could apprehend,
by some unpracticed sense, its mute significance.

Quaker Road

by Updike Farm; Princeton, New Jersey

There's a turn
in a New Jersey road
that leads to the flat lands
of Friesland
the farmed fields
of Harlingen and Heerenveen
stretch
to an expanse of sky
framed
by the road and long cut
of canal
soft-edged with willow
and wildwood
where water and clay
cloud and stone
meld, as in a painter's winter palette
—sluiced colors spilling
over loam
sweet water channels
mud-swept runnels
a shallow dig to sea.

Remembering Sally Topps

Guest of the Emperor, Tjideng Camp 1942-1945

Yesterday I dropped the last of Sally Topps's cups.
Too many shattered bits to mend, like fragments
of a torn postcard from the Far East scattered
over the Ijsselmeer—pieces of bone from a tiny Indonesian
woman I met once, alone in her basement flat in Amsterdam,
funky with bird feathers and hand-rolled cigarettes.

A rag doll who had meant something to someone long-gone
pressed upon me two plain French *bols de café*, a gift
to the newly wed, cracked along the rims even then.

Sally's story frozen into each grim crack, internment
during the war, forced to stand in the hot sun for hours,
interminable marches through the jungle
—a brown twig walking, a splinter of bamboo.
Her will become the insistent jungle hum,
her step mechanical as a mantis, bone on bone.

It was a legacy I did not want and yet,
once accepted, could not give up, a memory
evoked by the sight of glazed earthenware.

And so, I murmured each time I filled one with peanuts,
yogurt, cornflakes—*remember Sally Topps, how she survived.*

Child

After Lucy Sante

The first thing I saw was a round marble eye swimming in a milky sea. The first thing I saw was the red tongue of a great brown beast lapping at my eyelids. The first thing I saw was the edge of a stubble field, a cold gray ditch under a cold gray sky. The first thing I saw was cracked linoleum, a pile of old newspapers and an empty milk jug. The first thing I saw was a watery sky behind a broken skylight. The first thing I saw was a spider's web, houseflies parceled up in silk. The first thing I saw was the inside of a paper bag. The first thing I saw was the bright white teeth of my father's smile clenched around a fat cigar.

They sprinkled me with holy water. They stuffed me in a plastic sack and dropped me in the toilet. They tossed me off the Washington Bridge into the Hudson River. They suckled me with warm milk. They rocked me in my cradle, lullabied me, hush-a-bied me on a breaking bough. They ring-a-ring-a-rosied me, sold my skin for a rich widow's salve, my kidneys for a drunkard's spleen. They put me in a pumpkin shell. They left me alone in the cowshed. They taught me to count to ten, jump rope, shoot straight, play ball, stand tall, follow the leader, leapfrog, grin and bear it, take it on the chin. They made me dance for me mammy, sing for me daddy, cry like a baby, brave it like a man, pop the weasel, fetch a pail of water, sing a song of sixpence. They made me pick a pocketful of rhymes, rue the day that I was born. They broke my legs and made me a beggar. They baked me in a pie. They wrapped me in swaddling clothes and laid me in a manger. They smothered me with kindness, kissed away my tears, bought me penny candy and sugar tarts.

I climbed into a gingerbread house and found a thimble for a bed. I sailed the seven seas. I buckled my shoe, put my best foot forward and headed out West. I swept up the hair in my father's barber shop and, when he wasn't looking, I wove the snipped-off locks into a rope for my escape. I sold churros on the streets of Mexico City, pakoras on the streets of Delhi, hot tea in Lanzhou, 1000-year-old eggs in Canton. I shivered through desert nights on long caravan treks. I said my prayers like a dutiful child. I shoveled coals to Newcastle and picked through the dross for nuggets to ward off the winter chill. I lost my way and wound up in Red Rock Canyon outside a greyhound bus station waiting for a train. I learned to climb and pulled down a rainbow, but they said it would not do. I captured the castle, but the giant caught a glimpse of my shadow in the corner of his great green eye and lassoed me with a strand of my own hair. I roamed the world over with no suitcase and no plane ticket and only my two bare feet to carry me. I lived alone in the house that Jack built with a blind shrew for company.

Say hello to the boy who cried wolf. *Dit bonjour l'enfant sauvage*. Say good morning Curlylocks. Bring me strawberries and cream. Read me Homer and Goethe. Say come little one, cutiepie, mannikin. Remember me in your dreams. Think of me by the seashore, by the shining big sea water. Search for me in caverns underground, in the deep-delvèd earth, under cover of darkness, with a white bird as your guide. *Find me.*

Storm Over the Black Isle

Moniack Mhor, Inverness, Scotland, August 2024

Wind shook the slates last night
black feathers flailing
acorns battered against the ground like bursts of gunfire
the trees shivered—hurled a bird into the barn.

A harsh bird with no elegance.
It croaks and caws and makes demands.

I fear the melancholy in its eyes.
It will do me harm someday.

And yet I keep it, feed it.

Visitation

Last night my dead father came to me
Repeat after me, he said:
There is no loss here.
Repeat after me:
Who knows what memory will yield to the open heart.

In the morning, alter ego bids me speak
takes the bird from the stone

the bird flies backward
into memory, to find the tenement I loved
living in a bubble
with old souls in shawls.

Then they said:
Shhh, go to bed.
Here, put your slicker on and away outside to play.
They said:
Patch the pockets in these trousers.
Turn the collars on these shirts.
Run down to Smith's for a leek and some parsley.
Tell Grier the coalman I'll pay him next week.

Now they say:
Come inside, sit close, keep us warm.
Keep us alive.

Invitation

When was the last time
you walked barefoot
through wet grass?

Early morning cool
between your toes
soft mud squelching
at your balled step
your bold step
tripping through decades
of forgotten meadows.

Come.

One spring morning
when you wake to sunlight
tip-toe alone from dulling bed
disdain smug slippers.
Cross the threshold to green
and know each step as your own.

The Past

The past is cast skin
The past is a net of birds flung over treetops
The past is fabricated cloth drawn across thornbush
The past is laundered linen battered clean on river-rock, laid to dry
        on hedgerows
The past is prayer flags pegged on cotton ropes, whirligigged *en*
        masse on wire lines
The past is doubled-up excuses plastered on concrete, stuccoed
        imaginings
The past is petroglyphs crumbled into sand
The past is cracked photographs in shoeboxes, torn letters in a
        foreign tongue hidden between the pages of an old book
The past is words behind locked doors, muttered explanations,
        repeated siftings
The past is shifting images, *mirages*, curvesweep of geometry and sky
The past is half remembered hurts that shrink from sunlight
The past is *that bee sting when I was seven*
The past is inadequacies sloughed off with each retelling, as
        we reformulate the present, like snakes
        beginning with each skin-cast.

Just One Good Poem

After walking the D&R Greenway Poetry Trail, Princeton, New Jersey

Lord, let me have just one good poem. Just one.

Galway Kinnell's *Eating Blackberries.*
Couldn't you let me have one just like that?

Or the song about going back and forth all night on the ferry,
Yeats' *Lake Isle of Innisfree*, or Tennyson's perfect crimson petal.

What would it take? A right arm for Wright's *Blessing*?
I could do that. Certainly, for *If I Could Tell You*, I'd go that far.

For *I Will Make You Brooches* I'd gladly yield an ear, a toe, or two.
For *A Ritual to Read to Each Other* I'd part with an arm *and* a leg.

I'm not asking for an epic: *The Rime of the Ancient Mariner*,
Under Milk Wood or anything at all by your old friend Milton.

And I know it would be too much to wish for the likes of *Windhover*.
But oh, if I could write just one good poem before I'm done.

Something Mary Oliver might capture from the corner of her eye:
wild geese, high in the clean blue air, heading for home.

With Thanks

My thanks to all the editors who encouraged me: especially to Lois Marie Harrod and to the members of our poetry writing group: Susan Gerardi, Gail Mitchell, Chris Reed, Barbara Williams and Marie A. Wise; to the late Jean Hollander who inspired so many of us; and to Maria Mazziotti Gillan, Founder and Executive Director of the Poetry Center at Passaic County Community College in Paterson. I am also indebted to Vida Chu, fellow member of US1 Poets Cooperative and to Janie Herman at Princeton Public Library. Special thanks also to Jim Haba and John Glenday. Most recently, I have benefited from tutored retreats with Camilla Grudova, Genevieve Carver and Alycia Pirmohamed at Moniack Mhor, Scotland's National Writing Centre in Inverness.

Born and raised in the former mining village of Mossend in the central Lowlands of Scotland, **Linda Arntzenius** left home at 17 and took the train to London to follow a circuitous route into higher education, teaching and publishing, first in Bloomsbury and then in Los Angeles. She's taught in the departments of English at Mercer County Community College and The College of New Jersey and conducted an oral history project at the Institute for Advanced Study in Princeton. Her work has appeared in numerous online and print media. She spends several months of the year in Scotland and is a frequent visitor to Moniack Mhor, Scotland's National Writing Centre.

www.ingramcontent.com/pod-product-compliance
Lightning Source LLC
LaVergne TN
LVHW090540110826
845146LV00003B/1197

* 9 7 9 8 8 9 9 9 0 4 7 7 6 *